D0187159

MVFOL

EARNING MONEY

by Tanya Thayer

first step nonfiction

Lerner Publications Company · Minneapolis

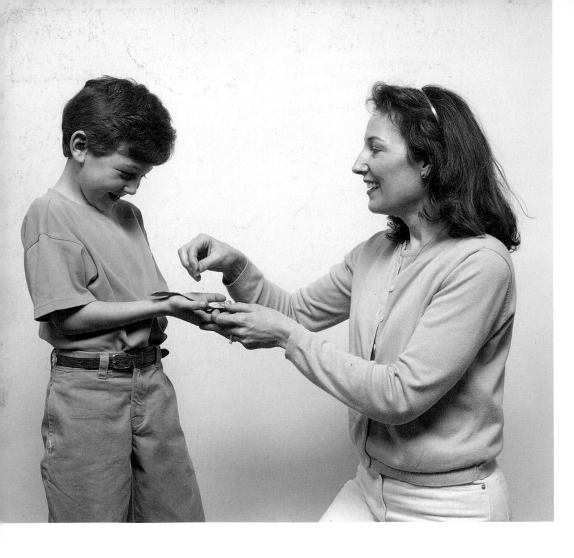

I can **earn money.**

When I **work** for money,
I earn it.

I can do my own **chores.**

I earn money when
I clean my room.

I can help my mom and
dad with chores.

I earn money when
I help my family.

I can do a **job.**

I earn money when
I wash cars.

I can sell things I don't
use anymore.

I earn money when
I sell my old bike.

I can make something.

I earn money when
I sell cookies.

I can grow something.

I earn money when
I sell vegetables.

I do many kinds of work.

I can earn money.

How Do Adults Earn Money?

Adults earn money working at their jobs. There are many kinds of jobs. Some people get paid to help others. Some people get paid to help run businesses. Some people get paid to make or grow things. Some people get paid to entertain us. What kinds of jobs are done by adults you know?

Earning Money

 Money doesn't grow on trees. What does this saying mean? It means that you have to work to get money; it doesn't just come to you by itself.

 Money that people earn can be taxed. Taxed money is used by the United States government to pay for things like public schools, roads, food for poor families, the military, and a lot more.

What is a service job?
A service job is any job where you do some kind of work for others. There are many service jobs. Being a doctor is a service job. Doctors earn money to keep people healthy. Plumbers fix people's pipes for money. And a mail carrier gets paid to bring people mail!

Glossary

 chores – jobs people do to keep their homes safe and clean

 earn – to get something for what you do

 job – the work someone has to do

 money – what people use to buy things

 work – the energy people use to do or make something

Index

The photographs in this book are reproduced through the courtesy of: SW Productions, front cover; Todd Strand/IPS, 2, 22 (2nd from top and 2nd from bottom); © Myrleen Ferguson Cate MRP/Photo Network, 3, 22 (bottom); © TRIP/S. Grant, 4, 22 (top); © Eric Anderson/Visuals Unlimited, 5; Corbis Royalty Free Images, 6, 12; © Jeff Greenberg/MR/Visuals Unlimited, 7; © Fotografia, Inc./CORBIS, 8, 22 (middle); © Seitz/Frozen/Photo Network, 9; © D. Yeske/ Visuals Unlimited, 10, 13; © Diane Meyer, 11, 17; © D. Cavagnaro/ Visuals Unlimited, 14; © Richard Thom/Visuals Unlimited, 15; © Stockbyte, 16.
Illustration on page 19 by Laura Westlund.

Lerner Publications Company
A division of Lerner Publishing Group
241 First Avenue North
Minneapolis, MN 55401 U.S.A.

Website address: www.lernerbooks.com

Library of Congress Cataloging-in-Publication Data

Thayer, Tanya.
        Earning money / by Tanya Thayer.
            p.   cm. — (First step nonfiction)
        Includes index.
        Summary: Presents ways a young child can earn money, such as doing chores or selling things.
        ISBN-13: 978–0–8225–1259–2 (lib. bdg. : alk. paper)
        ISBN-10: 0–8225–1259–9 (lib. bdg. : alk. paper)
        1. Money-making projects for children—Juvenile literature. 2. Entrepreneurship—Juvenile literature. 3. Children—Finance, Personal—Juvenile literature. [1. Moneymaking projects. 2. Entrepreneurship. 3. Finance, Personal.] I. Title. II. Series.
        HF5392 .T43 2003
        658'.041—dc21

Manufactured in the United States of America
3 4 5 6 7 8 – DP – 10 09 08 07 06 05

$4.25 USA

Money

Counting Money

Earning Money

Saving Money

Spending Money

First Step Nonfiction

A division of Lerner Publishing Group
www.lernerclassroom.com

ISBN 0-8225-1290-4

50425

9 780822 512905